WHAT THE

TRUMP?!

FIRST PUBLISHED IN THE UNITED KINGDOM
IN 2017 BY

PORTICO
43 GREAT ORMOND STREET
LONDON
WCIN 3HZ

AN IMPRINT OF PAVILION BOOKS COMPANY LTD

ISBN 9781911042785

A CIP CATALOGUE RECORD FOR THIS BOOK IS
AVAILABLE FROM THE BRITISH LIBRARY.

10 9 8 7 6 5 4 3 2 1 ...

PRINTED AND BOUND BY MARQUIS IN CANADA

DESIGNED AND ILLUSTRATED BY RORY LOWE.

THIS BOOK CAN BE ORDERED DIRECT FROM THE
PUBLISHER AT WWW.PAVILIONBOOKS.COM

WHAT THE

TRUMP?!

A SANE PERSON'S
GUIDE TO SURVIVING IN
THE AGE OF TRUMP.

BY STEVEN S. STEVENS

PORTICO

IT HAPPENED.

NO. BELIEVE IT...
IT REALLY HAPPENED.

THE LOCKER ROOM

USE THIS PAGE TO SAY WHATEVER
YOU LIKE. BE AS RACIST, SEXIST,
OFFENSIVE AND DOWNRIGHT
RIDICULOUS AS YOU CAN BE. IT'S
FINE, YOU'RE IN THE LOCKER ROOM.

TACKLING THE FIVE
STAGES OF GRIEF

1. ANGER

PLACE THIS PICTURE OF DONALD
TRUMP OVER SOMETHING SOFT
AND PUNCH IT REPEATEDLY UNTIL
YOU FEEL BETTER.

DE-CONSTRUCTING

DONALD

TAKE A LOOK AT THIS TRUMP
MASH-UP BELOW AND SEE IF IT
HELPS YOU COME TO TERMS
WITH PRESIDENT TRUMP'S PROS
AND CONS.

HANNIBAL

TRUMP

I.T. HELPDESK

HAS TRUMP'S PRESIDENCY
INFECTED YOUR SYSTEM?

TRY UNINSTALLING THE LATEST
TRUMP UPDATE (OR REINSTALL
OBAMASOFT 2.0).

ANXIETY ENEMA

CLIMATE CHANGE?

ASK BERNIE

DEAR UNCLE BERNIE,

I'VE GOT THIS COOL JOB RIGHT - BEEN THERE FOR 8 YEARS, THE JOB COMES WITH A HOUSE AND SERVANTS AND LIKE A COUNTRY AND STUFF. ME AND MY WIFE HAVE GOT IT JUST HOW WE WANT IT. BUT NOW MY JOB'S FINISHED AND WE HAVE TO LET THE NEW GUY LIVE HERE AND HE'S LIKE REALLY TACKY AND HE'S GONNA RUIN EVERYTHING. SHOULD I RIP IT ALL OUT OR LEAVE IT?

BARACK, WASHINGTON DC

UNCLE BERNIE SAYS:
JANEY, HAVE YOU SEEN MY GLASSES? DID YOU TAKE THEM FOR CLEANING AGAIN...

MELANIA'S WISDOM PEARLS

WHAT WOULD DONALD DO?

CONFIDENCE ISSUES? NOT SURE
YOU'VE GOT WHAT IT TAKES?
ASK YOURSELF:

WHAT WOULD DONALD DO?

• BE STRONG

• MAKE YOURSELF FEEL BETTER BY
BAD-MOUTHING ANYONE LESS
FORTUNATE THAN YOU

NOW - GO AND BUY
YOURSELF A NICE HOTEL!

BE CREATIVE

IMAGINE YOU ARE THE PRODUCER OF
THE LATEST TV SERIES TO BE
RE-BOOTED, 'THE A TEAM'!

WHO WILL YOU CAST TO PORTRAY
THEIR CRAZY ANTICS OVER THE
NEXT FOUR YEARS?

FACE ⟶ MIKE PENCE

HOWLING MAD
MURDOCK ⟶ GENERAL 'MAD
DOG' MATTIS

MR. T ⟶ MR. DONALD J. T.

HANNIBAL ⟶ VLAD PUTIN

THINK UP SOME IDEAS FOR STORY ARCS - USE THESE PROMPTS AS A STARTING POINT.

* THE A TEAM TRAVEL TO CHINA TO FIND PROOF THAT CLIMATE CHANGE REALLY IS A HOAX.

* THE A TEAM BUILD A HUGE WALL USING ONLY THE CONTENTS OF HANNIBAL'S SUITCASE TO KEEP OUT A GANG OF PESKY CRIMINALS.

* THE A TEAM HUNT DOWN A REALLY 'NASTY' WOMAN WHO HAS BEEN TAKING SECRET WORK HOME.

* THE A TEAM HAVE A REALLY GREAT BEACH HOLIDAY - THEY SURF, PLAY VOLLEYBALL. IT'S AS IF THE ONLY THING THAT MATTERS IN THE WORLD IS THEM, AND THEIR SPECIAL FRIENDSHIP. EVERYONE ELSE CAN GO TO HELL!!

MEDITATION MEDICATION

CLOSE YOUR EYES AND IMAGINE YOU
ARE IN A PLACE OF CALM AWAY
FROM THE MADNESS OF TRUMP. NOW
BUILD A WALL AROUND YOURSELF.
OH, MAYBE A FENCE?

OK, JUST EAT SOME ICE
CREAM AND HAVE A NAP.

LET IT GO!

JUMP AWAY YOUR ANGER
ON THIS TRUMPOLINE.

2020 VISION

STAY POSITIVE ABOUT THE FUTURE.
DRAW A ROSE IN THIS VASE,
BECAUSE THE FUTURE'S ROSY.*

*AS LONG AS YOU'RE NOT A
PERSON OF COLOUR, LGBT,
FEMALE, AN IMMIGRANT ETC.

TRUMP PET THERAPY

TRY TO MAKE TRUMP
MORE LOVABLE.

FEED A DONALD DUCK.

REWARD STATION

DID YOU AWAKE FROM A REVERIE
RECALLING A TIME WHEN POLITICS
DIDN'T RESEMBLE A CHEAP SOAP
OPERA AGAIN TODAY?

IF NOT THEN TREAT YOURSELF TO
AN EPISODE OF YOUR FAVOURITE
CHEAP SOAP OPERA.

EL PRESIDENTE OF

SANTA BARBARA

GET WHAT YOU PUTIN

SPEND SOME QUALITY TIME WITH
YOUR BEST BUDDY.

MAYBE PLAY A GAME OF CHINESE
WHISPERS AND SEE IF YOU CAN
WORK OUT CHINA'S SECRETS?

ELECTION DETOX

COUNTERBALANCE THE POISONOUS
ELECTION CAMPAIGN BY PURGING
YOURSELF OF YOUR INNER TOXINS
- GIVE UP ALCOHOL, FOR EXAMPLE.

ALTERNATIVELY, GET SO DRUNK
YOU FORGET WHO'S THE
PRESIDENT OF THE U.S.

CHALLENGE THE BRAIN

SPOT THE DIFFERENCE:

THE TRUMP WITHIN

WE ARE ALL CAPABLE OF BEING
RUTHLESS TYRANTS AT TIMES.
EVERY NOW AND THEN IT'S
GOOD TO BE BAD.

EMBRACE YOUR INNER DONALD!

HOW TO MAKE YOURSELF
GREAT AGAIN - TRUMP STYLE

SEND AN INSPIRATIONAL TWEET.

 DONALD J TRUMP ⊘   [FOLLOW]

I HAVE NEVER SEEN A THIN
PERSON DRINKING DIET COKE.

RETWEETS   LIKES
77,250   77,180

LEARN TO HAVE FUN AGAIN

TAKE YOUR MIND OFF YOUR
WORRIES, PLAN A DINNER FOR
FRIENDS USING THE MENU BELOW.

~~GUACAMOLE WITH TORTILLAS~~

AVOCADO SALAD WITH CHEETOS

◇

~~TRUMP STEAK~~

DUCK A L'ORANGE WITH BRAISED BABY
CARROTS AND SWEET POTATO

◇

TRUMPKIN PIE
WITH ALL-AMERICAN CREAM

◇

A CHOICE OF WHITE COFFEE

MIKE'S DIY

IMPROVE YOUR ENVIRONMENT THE MIKE PENCE WAY.

SCORE SOME BROWNIE POINTS BY PUTTING UP A WALL FOR THE BOSS.

SCORE EXTRA POINTS BY MAKING THE PEOPLE NEXT DOOR PAY FOR IT.

A NEW HOPE?

MAKE A LIST OF YOUR HOPES AND
FEARS FOR TRUMP'S PRESIDENCY.

FEARS:

_____

_____

_____

_____

_____

_____

_____

_____

_____

_____

HOPES:

_____

_____

HILLILEAKS

OPEN YOUR EYES TO THE SHOCKING
TRUTH ABOUT 'CROOKED' HILLARY
CLINTON.

THINGS TO BE

THANKFUL FOR

FOUR YEARS IS ONLY
1,461 SLEEPS.

PRESIDENTIAL WORD SEARCH

S	A	L	E	S	M	A	N	Y	L	L
E	L	S	T	S	I	P	A	R	G	I
M	A	S	S	H	O	L	E	R	P	A
S	E	X	I	S	T	P	Y	L	G	R
I	G	O	X	R	E	N	N	I	W	L
C	U	E	H	E	G	E	H	H	E	O
A	Y	R	E	V	X	X	I	G	K	H
R	X	B	S	O	Z	W	N	E	I	Y
L	P	M	S	B	O	A	O	R	S	F
A	Y	O	R	M	R	L	K	S	R	Q
R	T	H	Z	O	R	L	U	I	A	U
Y	O	M	B	C	P	P	C	C	H	D
H	I	L	L	A	R	Y	K	G	E	J

COMBOVER	ORANGE	SALESMAN
VERY	LIAR	RAPISTS
YUGE	WINNER	HOMBRE
WALL	HILLARY	RACISM
SEXIST	PUSSY	ASSHOLE

NEW FRIENDSHIPS

CHEER UP, MAKING NEW FRIENDS
MIGHT HELP PRESIDENT TRUMP TO
EMBRACE NEW IDEAS?

HOW ABOUT A
HUNKY, RICH
RUSSIAN OLIGARCH?

OR A YOUNG, MORE
FREE-SPIRITED
THINKER?

OR HOW ABOUT A
CRAZY BRIT WITH SOME
TIME ON HIS HANDS?

DISTRACTION ACTIONS

CAST AWAY YOUR WOES, FORGET
ABOUT TRUMP AND IMAGINE
YOURSELF IN THIS CALMING
ISLAND RETREAT.

THE STORY OF
TRUMPUNZEL

LULL YOURSELF TO SLEEP WITH THIS SOOTHING BEDTIME FAIRYTALE.

ONCE UPON A TIME IN THE FAIR OLD LAND
OF QUEENS, THERE LIVED A DASHING
YOUNG MAN CALLED TRUMPUNZEL. HIS
PARENTS WERE SO POOR THEY ONLY HAD $1
MILLION TO SPARE TO SET THE YOUNG
MAN OFF IN THE WORLD, BUT
NEVERTHELESS OFF HE WENT. SOON THE
ENTERPRISING TRUMPUNZEL CLAIMED HE HAD
AMASSED A MIGHTY $10 BILLION FORTUNE
(OR $3 BILLION DEPENDING ON WHO YOU
TALK TO). NO MATTER, TRUMPUNZEL WAS
RICH, BUT DESPITE THIS HE STILL WAS NOT
HAPPY. HE HAD ALREADY MARRIED AND
DIVORCED TWO OF THE FAIREST PRINCESSES
IN THE LAND, BUT ALL TO NO AVAIL.

DISCONSOLATE, TRUMPUNZEL TOOK HIMSELF OFF TO THE HIGHEST CHAMBER OF HIS HIGHEST TOWER, AND WEPT AND TOSSED AND TURNED. 'WHY DOES EVERYONE HATE ME' HE CRIED. WITH ALL THE WORRY TRUMPUNZEL BEGAN TO LOSE HIS BEAUTIFUL GOLDEN LOCKS, BUT AS HE LOST HAIR ON THE TOP OF HIS HEAD IT GREW MORE FULSOME AND LUSH AT THE SIDES, AND SOON HE HAD THE FINEST COMBOVER IN THE KINGDOM. BUT STILL HE WAS NOT HAPPY. ONE MORNING TRUMPUNZEL HEARD THE MOST BEAUTIFUL SINGING COMING FROM THE BOTTOM OF THE TOWER AND, ENCHANTED, HE CALLED DOWN. 'WHO IS IT THAT SINGS SO SWEETLY?'

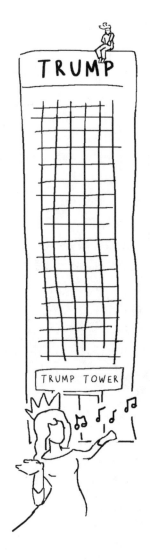

'IT IS I, PRINCESS MELANIA' CAME
THE MELODIOUS REPLY.
TRUMPUNZEL DETECTED A
FOREIGN ACCENT IN HER VOICE,
BUT DESPITE HIS FORTHRIGHT
VIEWS ON IMMIGRATION HE
DECIDED TO RISK A MEETING, AND
WITH THAT HE UNFURLED HIS
COLOSSAL COMBOVER,
UNRAVELLING IT THE FULL
LENGTH OF THE TOWER.
WITHOUT HESITATION THE
PLUCKY PRINCESS CLIMBED UP
THE TANGLED TRESS AND SOON
WAS PULLING HERSELF OVER THE
PRECIPICE AND INTO THE ARMS
OF OUR HERO. TRUMPUNZEL
FELL INSTANTLY IN LOVE, AND
DESPITE HIS CRACKPOT IDEAS,
FASCISTIC POLITICS AND
RIDICULOUS HAIRSTYLE, MELANIA
SOMEHOW FOUND IT IN HER
HEART TO LOVE THE MUCH
OLDER MULTI-BILLIONAIRE. SOON
THEY WERE MARRIED AND LIVED
HAPPILY EVER AFTER. THEY LIVED
HAPPILY EVER AFTER!!

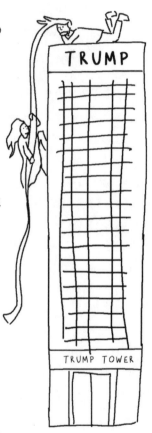

THE END

CONSOLATION HUG

DON'T FEEL ASHAMED OR
EMBARRASSED TO BE UPSET AT
TRUMP'S PRESIDENTIAL VICTORY,
YOU'RE NOT ALONE. AFTER ALL —
EVEN THE REPUBLICAN PARTY DIDN'T
WANT TRUMP TO WIN.

CUDDLE YOURSELF.

TRUMP L'OEIL

THE FRENCH TERM TROMPE L'OEIL
TRANSLATED MEANS TO 'DECEIVE
THE EYE'. HONE YOUR POWERS OF
PERCEPTION TO DECIDE WHAT IS
TRUTH AND WHAT IS NOT FROM
THE STATEMENT BELOW:

'ALL OF THE WOMEN ON THE
APPRENTICE FLIRTED WITH ME -
CONSCIOUSLY OR UNCONSCIOUSLY,
THAT'S TO BE EXPECTED.'

TRUMP: HOW TO GET RICH, 2004

TRUE   FALSE

ACTIVITY CORNER

FIND TIME TO RELAX. PLAY WITH
SOME RUSSIAN DONALDS.

THE BIGGER THE DOLL – THE MORE
POMPOUS HE LOOKS!

DRAIN THE SWAMP

TAKE CONTROL OF YOUR OWN
DESTINY AND RID YOURSELF OF
FAKE NEWS, TROLLING AND
ONLINE NEGATIVITY.

DRAIN THE POWER FROM YOUR SMART
PHONE AND SMASH IT TO SMITHEREENS
WITH A SLEDGEHAMMER.

BE INVENTIVE

THINK OF SOME USES FOR
MIKE PENCE.

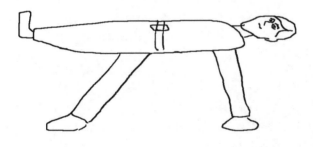

IRONING BOARD. YOU CAN IRON
YOUR UNDERWEAR ON HIM.

AMERICA'S NEXT

TOP PRESIDENT

DONALD TRUMP HAS PROVED THAT
LITERALLY ANYONE CAN BE
PRESIDENT OF THE USA.
ENGAGE YOUR IMAGINATION BY
ENVISIONING WHO MIGHT BE NEXT:

ELMO

SIMON
COWELL

HANNIBAL
LECTER

TACKLING THE FIVE
STAGES OF GRIEF

2. DENIAL

FACE YOUR GRIEF.
DONALD TRUMP IS THE PRESIDENT
OF THE UNITED STATES OF
AMERICA. THAT'S NOT GOING TO
CHANGE, NO MATTER HOW MANY
DOUGHNUTS YOU EAT!

DE-CONSTRUCTING DONALD

TAKE A LOOK AT THIS TRUMP
MASH-UP BELOW AND SEE IF IT
HELPS YOU COME TO TERMS
WITH PRESIDENT TRUMP'S PROS
AND CONS.

DALAI

TRUMP

I.T. HELPDESK

HAS TRUMP'S PRESIDENCY
INFECTED YOUR SYSTEM?

VIRUS ALERT!

YOUR COMPUTER HAS BEEN HIJACKED
BY A MALICIOUS PRESIDENT!

ANXIETY ENEMA

GUN CONTROL?

ASK BERNIE

DEAR UNCLE BERNIE,

I'VE GONE AND GOT MYSELF INTO A TERRIBLE MESS. I TOLD A WHOLE BUNCH OF YUGE LIES AS A JOKE AND EVERYONE BELIEVED ME. NOW I'VE GOT TO RUN THE COUNTRY. I'M OUT OF MY DEPTH. HELP!

ANONYMOUS, WASHINGTON DC

UNCLE BERNIE SAYS: WHAT'S THAT? IS THERE SOMEONE THERE? JANEY - THAT BOY FROM NEXT DOOR IS TAUNTING ME AGAIN.

MELANIA'S WISDOM PEARLS

WHAT WOULD DONALD DO?

ARE YOU SADDENED BY THE HURTFUL THINGS OTHER PEOPLE SAY? ASK YOURSELF:

WHAT WOULD DONALD DO?

- PLUG YOUR EARS

- NEVER LISTEN TO YOUR CRITICS, EVEN WHEN THEY'RE RIGHT

NOW TREAT YOURSELF TO A SPA DAY!

TANGERINE ULTRA FAKE TAN

LET IT GO!

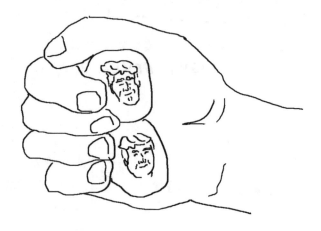

RELIEVE YOUR STRESS BY SQUEEZING
A PAIR OF TRUMP BALLS.

TACKLING THE FIVE
STAGES OF GRIEF

3. DEPRESSION

CHEER UP! IT MIGHT NEVER HAPPEN.

OH WAIT...

TRUMP PET THERAPY

TRY TO MAKE TRUMP LOVABLE

STROKE A TRUMP PUSSY

2020 VISION

STAY POSITIVE ABOUT THE FUTURE.
DRAW A RAY OF HOPE ON THE SUN:

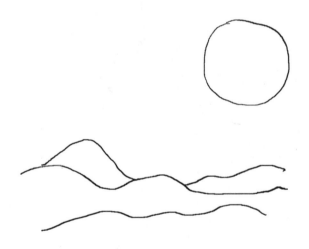

DON'T WORRY - IT WON'T MELT
ANY ICECAPS, BECAUSE APPARENTLY
CLIMATE CHANGE ISN'T A THING.

HAIR TODAY...

STYLE YOUR OWN
TRUMP COMBOVER.

GET WHAT YOU PUTIN

SPEND SOME QUALITY TIME WITH
YOUR BEST FRIEND.

MAYBE STRIP OFF AND WRESTLE A
RUSSIAN BEAR.

REWARD STATION

DID YOU FIND YOURSELF FANTASISING
THAT BARACK OBAMA WAS STILL THE
MOST POWERFUL MAN IN THE
WORLD? NO? THEN YOU'RE
RECOVERING. REWARD YOURSELF WITH
A TRUMP STEAK.

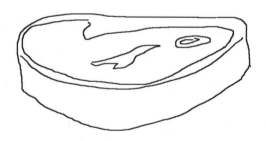

ELECTION DETOX

CUT OUT ALL THE POISONOUS
RHETORIC BELOW AND PLACE THEM
CAREFULLY IN THE TOILET. NOW EAT
NOTHING BUT KALE SMOOTHIES FOR
A WEEK, AND FLUSH ALL THAT
TOXICITY AWAY!

'NASTY WOMAN!'

'OBAMA'S BIRTH CERTIFICATE IS A FRAUD!'

'BUILD A WALL!'

'DRUG DEALERS, CRIMINALS AND RAPISTS!'

'LOCK HER UP!'

CHALLENGE THE BRAIN

SPOT THE
DIFFERENCE:

1.

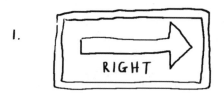

RIGHT

2.

ALT

RIGHT

TRANSCEND DEFEAT

IF YOU'RE STILL REELING FROM
TRUMP'S VICTORY THERE'S AN EASY
WAY TO KEEP THE DREAM ALIVE:

GO TO SLEEP FOR THE NEXT
FOUR YEARS.

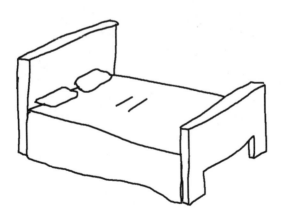

HOW TO MAKE YOURSELF
GREAT AGAIN - TRUMP STYLE

THROW AWAY EVERYTHING THAT
WASN'T MADE IN THE USA.

YOU'LL LOSE YOUR CAR, CLOTHES
AND TECHNOLOGY.
BUT YOU'LL BE BETTER.

WORRY WAGON

THE OUTLAW WILD DONNIE TRUMP
HAS LOADED UP THE WORRY
WAGON WITH ALL YOUR ANXIETIES.

YOU'RE THE SHERIFF - DRIVE THE
WAGON OVER THE CLIFF AND SLAM
THE OUTLAW IN THE CELLS.

MIKE'S DIY

IMPROVE YOUR ENVIRONMENT THE

MIKE PENCE WAY.

BUILD A SANDPIT FOR THE KIDS.

FILL IT WITH SAND.

NOW BURY YOUR HEAD IN

IT UNTIL 2020.

LEARN TO SPEAK TRUMP

FROM UNDERSTANDING
COMES FORGIVENESS.

GINA $\longrightarrow$ CHINA

YUGE $\longrightarrow$ HUGE

VERY VERY VERY $\longrightarrow$ VERY

RIGGED $\longrightarrow$ FAIR

BAD HOMBRE $\longrightarrow$ MEXICAN

NASTY WOMAN $\longrightarrow$ WOMAN

GRAB $\longrightarrow$ SEIZE SUDDENLY

WALL $\longrightarrow$ FENCE

FENCE $\longrightarrow$ METAPHORICAL DIVIDE

HILLILEAKS

· OPEN YOUR EYES TO THE SHOCKING TRUTH ABOUT 'CROOKED' HILLARY CLINTON.

SAY GOODBYE

PROPERLY GRIEVE AND MOVE
ON FROM THESE SAD
LOSSES IN 2016:

- DAVID BOWIE
- ALAN RICKMAN
- PRINCE
- MUHAMMAD ALI
- GENE WILDER
- LEONARD COHEN
- AMERICAN SANITY AND INTEGRITY

THINGS TO BE
THANKFUL FOR

THERE'S ONLY ONE DONALD
TRUMP. AND HUMAN CLONING
ISN'T A THING YET.

LET IT GO

DRAW DONALD TRUMP'S FACE ON
A BIG ORANGE BALLOON.

NOW TAKE IT OUTSIDE, LET IT
GO AND WATCH ALL YOUR ANGER
FLOAT AWAY.

ALTERNATIVELY, JUST POP IT WITH
A LARGE, SHARP PIN.

DISTRACTION ACTIONS

CAST AWAY YOUR WOES, FORGET ABOUT TRUMP AND BOOK YOURSELF A REPLENISHING, FIVE-STAR, LUXURY CITY BREAK,

NATURE'S REMEDY

PLANT A SEED. WATER IT
EVERY DAY AND WATCH IT
GROW. FEEL ITS ENERGY.

NOW SMOKE IT UNTIL EVERYTHING
FEELS ALRIGHT AGAIN.

RESTORE YOUR FAITH

PUT A BAND-AID ON THE
IMAGE BELOW TO MEND YOUR
BROKEN HEART.

I

USA

INFLATE YOUR EGO

PUT THESE EARPLUGS IN YOUR EARS,
SO THAT YOU CAN BE COMPLETELY
IMMUNE TO ALL CRITICISM.

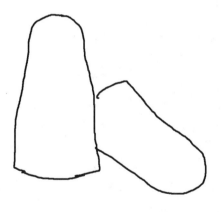

BREATHE

NOW HOLD THAT FOR AT
LEAST FOUR YEARS.

TRUMP L'OEIL

HONE YOUR POWERS OF PERCEPTION
TO DECIDE WHAT IS TRUTH AND
WHAT IS NOT FROM THE
STATEMENT BELOW:

'I THINK I'M A VERY HONEST GUY,
AND IN FACT, MAYBE TOO HONEST TO
BE A POLITICIAN.'

- TRUMP ON LATE EDITION WITH WOLF BLITZER
28TH NOV 1999

TRUE   FALSE

THIS IS NOT
A DREAM

AND IF IT WAS IT WOULD NEED TO
LAST A MINIMUM OF FOUR YEARS.
AND EVEN THEN IT WOULD BE A
VERY DISTRESSING NIGHTMARE.

STRESS-BUSTERS

TAKE YOUR DOG FOR A NICE, RELAXING WALK.

AMERICA'S NEXT
TOP PRESIDENT

ENGAGE YOUR IMAGINATION BY
ENVISIONING AN UNLIKELIER
PRESIDENT THAN THE DONALD:

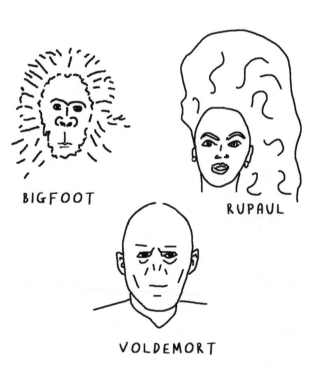

BIGFOOT

RUPAUL

VOLDEMORT

LOCKER ROOM TALK

SAY WHAT YOU WANT, ANYTHING
GOES, YOU'RE IN THE LOCKER ROOM!

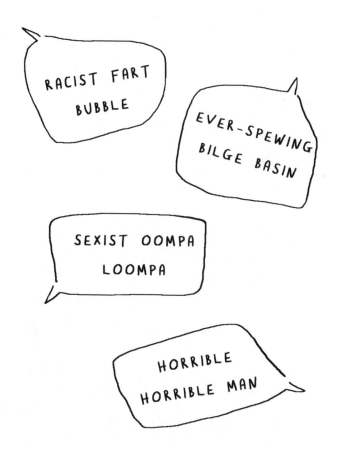

EMBRACE CHANGE

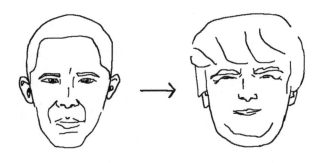

ORANGE IS THE NEW BLACK

BE INVENTIVE

THINK OF SOME USES FOR
MIKE PENCE.

STREET LIGHT

I.T. HELPDESK

HAS TRUMP'S PRESIDENCY
INFECTED YOUR SYSTEM?

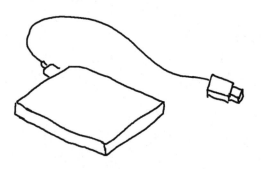

SIMPLY RESTORE FROM A
PREVIOUS BACKUP. (YOU DID
MAKE A BACKUP, DIDN'T YOU?!)

DE-CONSTRUCTING DONALD

TAKE A LOOK AT THIS TRUMP
MASH-UP BELOW AND SEE IF IT
HELPS YOU COME TO TERMS
WITH PRESIDENT TRUMP'S PROS
AND CONS.

KIM
TRUMP-UN

ANXIETY ENEMA

FREE HEALTHCARE?

ASK BERNIE

SECRET LOVE

DEAR UNCLE BERNIE,

I'M WORKING WITH THIS GUY AND IT'S REALLY AMAZING. HE'S NOT AFRAID TO MAKE OUTRAGEOUS COMMENTS AND SOMETIMES HE MAKES ME GASP – HE'S SO EXCITING. I TRY TO BE LIKE HIM BUT I ALWAYS END UP LOOKING LIKE A DOOFUS. HE HAS FANTASTIC HAIR AND HE MAKES ME FEEL FIZZY IN MY BELLY. IS THIS WRONG?

MIKE, INDIANA

UNCLE BERNIE SAYS:
THIS OATMEAL IS GOOD TODAY, JANEY. SET ME UP FOR MY NAP.

MELANIA'S WISDOM PEARLS

WHAT WOULD DONALD DO?

FEELING OUT OF YOUR DEPTH?
WORRIED YOU CAN'T LIVE UP
TO THE PROMISES YOU MADE?
ASK YOURSELF:

WHAT WOULD DONALD DO?

- MAKE NEW, EASIER PROMISES

- PRETEND YOU KNOW WHAT
  YOU'RE DOING

NOW - PLAY A FEW ROUNDS
OF GOLF. OR MAYBE BUY
THE WHOLE COURSE?

LET IT GO

TURN THAT NEGATIVE ENERGY
INTO A POSITIVE, BASH THE
HELL OUT OF THIS TRUMP...

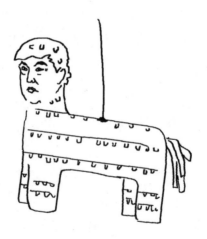

PIÑATA.

TACKLING THE FIVE
STAGES OF GRIEF

4. BARGAINING

TRY NOT TO FIXATE ON
REVERSING THE DECISION.
BIT LATE NOW ANYWAY...
PERHAPS IF CLINTON HAD DONE AS
MUCH BARGAINING AS TRUMP WE
WOULDN'T BE IN THIS HOLE NOW.

BE PROACTIVE

ARRANGE AN ANTI-TRUMP PROTEST.
CAN YOU THINK OF ANY BANNERS?

HERE ARE A FEW TO START
YOU OFF:

REWARD STATION

DO YOU FIND YOURSELF
PRETENDING HILLARY WON THE
PRESIDENTIAL ELECTION?
IF YES THEN CARRY ON. THAT IS
ABOUT AS GOOD AS IT'S GONNA
GET. THAT IS YOUR REWARD.

TRUMP PET THERAPY

TRY TO MAKE DONALD
MORE LOVABLE

CUDDLE A CHEEKY TRUMPANZEE

2020 VISION

STAY POSITIVE ABOUT
THE FUTURE.

HERE'S A TUNNEL.

DRAW A LIGHT AT
THE END OF IT.

GET WHAT YOU PUTIN

SPEND SOME QUALITY TIME WITH
YOUR BEST FRIEND.

PUT THE WORLD TO RIGHTS OVER
A BOTTLE OF RUSSIAN VODKA.

ELECTION DETOX

DRIVE OUT TO THE COUNTRY. FIND
A SECLUDED SPOT AWAY FROM
ANYONE AT ALL. TAKE A DEEP
BREATH OF PURE, FRESH AIR AND
MARVEL AT THE PEACEFULNESS
AROUND YOU.

NOW STAY THERE UNTIL 2020.

CHALLENGE

THE BRAIN

SPOT THE DIFFERENCE:

1.

2.

METAPHORICAL WALL

R.E.S.P.E.C.T.

OBAMA
GLOBAL
RESPECT

DIVIDE
BY 100

MINIMUM GLOBAL
RESPECT NEEDED
FOR POTUS

TRUMP
GLOBAL
RESPECT

MULTIPLY
BY 100

HOW TO MAKE YOURSELF
GREAT AGAIN - TRUMP STYLE

LEARN A MAGIC TRICK TO MAKE ALL
YOUR TAX BILLS DISAPPEAR!

PICK YOUR SPOTS

JOIN THESE DOTS IN ANY WAY YOU
LIKE. WHATEVER PATTERN FORMS
SUGGESTS WHAT YOU ARE
CURRENTLY WORRYING ABOUT.

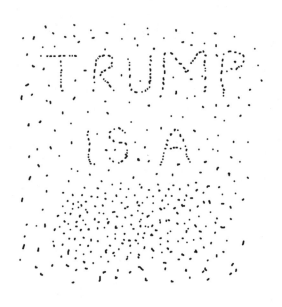

WHAT IMAGES PRESENT THEMSELVES?

MIKE'S DIY

ENJOY YOUR ENVIRONMENT THE

MIKE PENCE WAY.

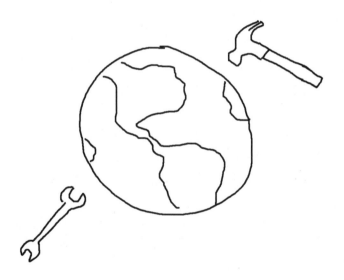

CREATE A PLANET AND ALL LIFE

ON IT IN JUST SEVEN DAYS.

ORDER YOUR THOUGHTS

MAKE A LIST OF ALL THE
NEGATIVE POINTS ABOUT
TRUMP'S RISE TO POWER:

_____

_____

_____

_____

_____

_____

_____

_____

_____

_____

NOW THE POSITIVES:

_____

HILLILEAKS

OPEN YOUR EYES TO THE
SHOCKING TRUTH ABOUT 'CROOKED'
HILLARY CLINTON.

ROUTINE CHANGE

COMPLETE THIS LIST OF WAYS TO
CHANGE YOUR DAILY ROUTINE:

- HAVE A WORK FRIEND AROUND FOR DINNER

- CHANGE YOUR BRAND OF COFFEE

- TAKE A DIFFERENT ROUTE TO WORK

- ADJUST TO THE FACT THAT THE
LEADER OF THE FREE WORLD IS AN
EGOTISTICAL MEGALOMANIAC

-

-

-

-

THINGS TO BE
THANKFUL FOR

DONALD TRUMP DOESN'T
HAVE A DEATHSTAR...

...YET!

MAC TRUMP

DE-STRESS WITH SOME ART THERAPY

COLOUR IN THIS TARTAN ORANGE

DISTRACTION ACTIONS

CAST AWAY YOUR WOES,
FORGET ABOUT TRUMP AND
RELAX IN FRONT OF THE TV.

THE STORY OF TRUMPELSTILTSKIN

LULL YOURSELF TO SLEEP WITH THIS SOOTHING BEDTIME FAIRYTALE.

ONCE UPON A TIME IN THE FARAWAY LAND OF AMERICA THERE LIVED AN AMBITIOUS OLD DAMSEL NAMED LADY HILLARY. SHE WAS JEALOUS OF HER HUSBAND LORD BILL WHO HAD AT ONE TIME BEEN THE MOST POPULAR COURTIER IN THE LAND (DESPITE HIS LYING AND INFIDELITY). ALTHOUGH LADY HILLARY WORKED VERY HARD AT KING OBAMA'S COURT (EVEN TAKING TOP-SECRET SCROLLS HOME WITH HER TO WORK ON AT NIGHT), SHE WAS STILL VERY UNPOPULAR WITH THE PEOPLE OF THE REALM.

ONE DAY KING OBAMA ANNOUNCED HE WAS TO ABDICATE. HE HAD GROWN WEARY OF FRUITLESSLY TRYING TO PUSH THROUGH PROGRESSIVE POLICIES. THERE WAS TO BE A NEW KING AND ANYONE COULD APPLY. SO A ROYAL DECREE WAS SENT OUT TO THE FOUR CORNERS OF THE LAND.

PROUD LADY HILLARY ANNOUNCED HER CANDIDACY.
AFTER ALL, SHE WAS BY FAR THE MOST QUALIFIED
AND EXPERIENCED TO RUN THE COUNTRY, DESPITE
HER LACK OF LIKABILITY. JUST THEN, A STRANGE-
LOOKING FELLOW WITH FLAXEN LOCKS PILED
UPON HIS HEAD STEPPED FORWARD AND BOWED
BEFORE THE KING.

'MY NAME IS TRUMPELSTILTSKIN,' SPAT THE
TANGERINE-TINGED OLD MAN, 'AND I HEREBY
DECLARE MY CANDIDACY. FURTHERMORE, SHOULD I
BECOME KING, I WILL ENSURE THAT LADY HILLARY
IS THROWN INTO PRISON FOR BEING NASTY!'
WANTING TO PREVENT THIS CRUSTY OLD LOON
FROM BECOMING KING, OBAMA THOUGHT ON HIS
FEET. 'WHOMEVER BRINGS ME THE MOST GOLD BY
DAYBREAK WILL BE MY SUCCESSOR,' HE TOLD HIS
COURTIERS. BUT THE CLEVER KING SECRETLY
THREW THE NOXIOUS SEPTUAGENARIAN INTO THE
DUNGEON WITH ONLY A RUSTY OLD SPINNING
WHEEL TO KEEP HIM COMPANY.

NOW, READER, YOU MAY BE FEELING SORRY FOR
TRUMPELSTILTSKIN? BUT WHAT YOU DON'T KNOW,
OR WHAT LADY HILLARY DIDN'T KNOW, NOR
INDEED THE KING FOR THAT MATTER WAS THAT
THIS OLD MAN WAS THE RICHEST MAN IN THE
LAND. AND THE SOURCE OF THIS WEALTH WAS
HIS MAGIC COMBOVER WHICH, WHEN SPUN IN A
SPINNING WHEEL, PRODUCED THE FINEST GOLD
THREAD. SO ALL THROUGH THE NIGHT, THE OLD
GEEZER SPUN HIS FLAXEN LOCKS, AND WHEN HE
WAS RELEASED AT DAYBREAK HE PRESENTED HIS
GOLDEN BOUNTY. KING OBAMA HAD NO CHOICE
BUT TO MAKE TRUMPELSTILTSKIN THE NEW KING
OF ALL AMERICA.
THE CROWD CHEERED AS TRUMPELSTILTSKIN THREW
LADY HILLARY INTO CHAINS AND REVERSED ALL OF
THE KINDLY KING OBAMA'S ROYAL DECREES.

THE END

BE HERE NOW

SIT COMPLETELY STILL, BREATHE
DEEPLY AND CLEAR YOUR MIND. IT'S
HARD BUT TRY TO EMPTY YOUR HEAD
OF ALL THOUGHTS COMPLETELY.

DON'T THINK ABOUT OTHER PEOPLE.

DON'T THINK ABOUT OTHER PLACES.

TURN OFF YOUR EMPATHY AND THINK
ONLY OF YOURSELF FOR ONCE.

GREAT ISN'T IT! NOW YOU KNOW
HOW IT FEELS TO BE THE DONALD.

TRUMP L'OEIL

HONE YOUR POWERS OF PERCEPTION
TO DECIDE WHAT IS TRUTH AND
WHAT IS NOT FROM THE
STATEMENT BELOW:

'AN EXTREMELY CREDIBLE SOURCE HAS
CALLED MY OFFICE AND TOLD ME
THAT @BARACKOBAMA'S BIRTH
CERTIFICATE IS A FRAUD.'

– TWITTER, @REALDONALDTRUMP,
1.23PM 6 AUG 2012

TRUE   FALSE

SPREAD THE LOVE

DRAW A WARM SMILE ON HILLARY TO CHEER HER UP AND IMPROVE HER LIKABILITY.

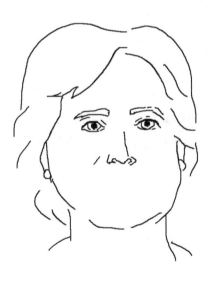

BE INVENTIVE

THINK OF SOME USES FOR
MIKE PENCE.

A HAT STAND PERHAPS?

YOU COULD HANG YOUR SLOGAN
CAPS ON HIM?

LET IT GO

TAKE A LUMP OF ORANGE
MODELLING CLAY AND MOULD IT
INTO TRUMP'S FACE. NOW TAKE A
ROLLING PIN AND CAREFULLY BASH
THE FACE REPEATEDLY UNTIL IT'S A
LUMP AGAIN.

A LUMP OF TRUMP.

AMERICA'S NEXT

TOP PRESIDENT

ENGAGE YOUR IMAGINATION BY
ENVISIONING AN UNLIKELIER
PRESIDENT THAN THE DONALD:

'GANGNAM STYLE'
PSY

KIM
KARDASHIAN

DARTH VADER, LORD
OF THE SITH

LOCKER ROOM TALK

SAY WHAT YOU WANT, ANYTHING GOES, YOU'RE IN THE LOCKER ROOM!

I.T. HELPDESK

HAS TRUMP'S PRESIDENCY
INFECTED YOUR SYSTEM?

HAVE YOU TRIED TURNING IT OFF
AND ON AGAIN? REBOOT TRUMP OUT
OF THE WHITE HOUSE!

DE-CONSTRUCTING DONALD

TAKE A LOOK AT THIS TRUMP
MASH-UP BELOW AND SEE IF IT
HELPS YOU COME TO TERMS
WITH PRESIDENT TRUMP'S PROS
AND CONS.

DONALD

MANDELA

ANXIETY ENEMA

WORLD PEACE?

I JUST DON'T GIVE A DONALD

ASK BERNIE

DEAR UNCLE BERNIE,

HOW CAN I STOP FEELING LIKE SUCH A BIG FAT LOSER? I WANTED THE CHANCE TO GET MY DREAM JOB BUT INSTEAD THEY GAVE IT TO THE MOST RIDICULOUS CANDIDATE IMAGINABLE. I EVEN TRIED TO BE COOL AND THAT DIDN'T WORK. WORSE STILL IS THAT MY HUSBAND USED TO DO THIS JOB AND HE'S A COMPLETE NUMBNUT. WHY WON'T THEY LET ME BE PRESIDENT?

HILLARY, NYC

UNCLE BERNIE SAYS:
JANEY - HAVE YOU MOVED MY SLIPPERS? WHO KEEPS TOUCHING MY SLIPPERS? GEEZ!

MELANIA'S WISDOM PEARLS

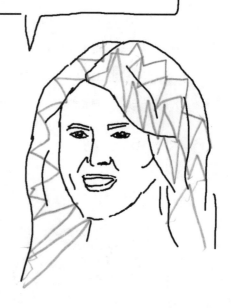

WHAT WOULD DONALD DO?

FEELING STRESSED? GOT THE
WORLD ON YOUR SHOULDERS?
ASK YOURSELF:

WHAT WOULD DONALD DO?

- BELIEVE IN YOURSELF, NO
  MATTER HOW CRAZY YOUR IDEAS

- BLAME EVERYONE ELSE FOR YOUR
  OWN MISTAKES

NOW - RELAX AND ENJOY SOME
NICE, HEALTHY FOOD.

LET IT GO

PLACE YOUR BUTT ON THIS
TRUMP-HOPPER AND BOUNCE
AWAY YOUR FRUSTRATION.

TACKLING THE FIVE
STAGES OF GRIEF

5. ACCEPTANCE

LOOK. JUST DEAL WITH IT. WHY
NOT PAINT YOURSELF ORANGE,
PUT A DEAD FOX ON YOUR HEAD
AND GET ON WITH IT!

BE CREATIVE

GET YOUR MOJO GOING AGAIN –
IMAGINE YOU ARE A TOP
HOLLYWOOD PRODUCER WHO HAS
BEEN GREENLIT TO MAKE A MOVIE
ABOUT TRUMP. WHAT MIGHT YOU
CALL IT?

HERE'S A FEW IDEAS...

- THE TRUMPINATOR – HASTA LA
  VISTA, DONALD

- THE SOUND OF MUSIC II – THE VON
  TRUMP FAMILY TAKE WASHINGTON

- ORANGEFINGER

- TRUMPAGEDDON

- FORREST TRUMP

- THE LADY AND THE TRUMP

WHO MIGHT YOU CAST AS THE MAIN CHARACTERS?

DONALD TRUMP
- ROBERT REDFORD
- ALEC BALDWIN
- KOJAK

HILLARY CLINTON
- MERYL STREEP
- KATE MCKINNON
- SOMEONE POPULAR

BARACK OBAMA
- WILL SMITH
- DENZEL WASHINGTON
- WILL SMITH

BERNIE SANDERS
- DUSTIN HOFFMAN
- WOODY ALLEN
- YODA

MIKE PENCE
- CLINT EASTWOOD
- SIR IAN MCKELLEN
- A PLANK OF WOOD

TRUMP PET THERAPY

TRY TO MAKE DONALD LOVABLE

AHH... A CUTE TRUMP CHIHUAHUA.
GIVE THAT 'BAD HOMBRE' A HUG

↓

CHANGE YOUR
PERSPECTIVE*

*MOVE TO MARS

2020 VISION

STAY POSITIVE ABOUT
THE FUTURE.

HERE'S A CLOUD.

DRAW A SILVER LINING.

GET WHAT YOU PUTIN

SPEND SOME QUALITY TIME WITH YOUR BEST BUDDY. MAYBE HAVE A SLEEPOVER AT THE KREMLIN.

STAY UP ALL NIGHT EATING FAST FOOD, PLAYING TETRIS AND TELLING SCARY STORIES ABOUT POOR PEOPLE.

ANGER TRUMPET

IGNITE YOUR EMOTIONS AND RATIONALISE YOUR FEELINGS. HOW DOES THIS IMAGE MAKE YOU FEEL?

IF AT FIRST YOU

DON'T SUCCEED

BE LIKE DONALD! DON'T GIVE UP –
EVEN WITH A STRING OF
FAILURES BEHIND YOU...

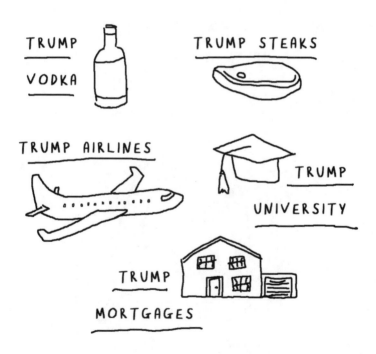

TRUMP
VODKA

TRUMP STEAKS

TRUMP AIRLINES

TRUMP
UNIVERSITY

TRUMP
MORTGAGES

AIM FOR PRESIDENT!
ANYONE CAN DO IT.

HOW TO MAKE YOURSELF
GREAT AGAIN - TRUMP STYLE

YOU'D LOOK GREAT IN A NICE NEW
HAT - MAYBE SOMETHING IN RED?

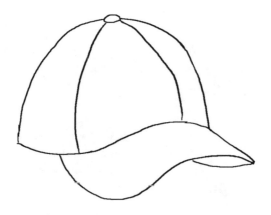

CHALLENGE THE BRAIN

SPOT THE DIFFERENCE:

1.

2.

ANSWER: 1.23% DNA

DIFFERENTIAL

PHILOSOPHY COUCH

DID BARACK OBAMA

ACTUALLY EVER EXIST?

DISCUSS...

PUSSY GRAB

NO JOKE HERE

MIKE'S DIY

IMPROVE YOUR ENVIRONMENT THE
MIKE PENCE WAY.

PICK UP SOME TIMBER AND BUILD A
LARGE CRATE.

DRILL SOME HOLES IN IT FOR AIR.
NOW CLIMB INTO IT AND STAY
THERE UNTIL SOMEONE NOTICES.

HILLILEAKS

OPEN YOUR EYES TO THE SHOCKING
TRUTH ABOUT 'CROOKED' HILLARY
CLINTON.

RELAX

DE-STRESS WITH SOME
COLOURING IN.

COLOUR THIS WHITE HOUSE ORANGE.

THINGS TO BE
THANKFUL FOR

MIKE PENCE IS STILL
ONLY VICE PRESIDENT.

YOU'RE HIRED!

IMAGINE YOU'RE A GO-GETTING ENTREPRENEUR. PITCH AN UNREFUSABLE BUSINESS-PLAN TO PRESIDENT TRUMP.

HERE ARE SOME EXAMPLES TO GET YOU GOING.

- TRUMP TANKS

- TRUMP BARBED WIRE

- TRUMP NUCLEAR WARHEADS

-

-

-

-

DISTRACTION ACTIONS

CAST AWAY YOUR WOES, FORGET ABOUT TRUMP AND IMMERSE YOURSELF IN THIS BEAUTIFUL LANDSCAPE OF THE MANHATTAN SKYLINE.

RESTORE YOUR FAITH

MEND THIS BROKEN POLITICAL
SYSTEM BY PUTTING THE PIECES
BACK TOGETHER.

NATURE'S REMEDY

PLANT A SEED. WATER IT
EVERY DAY AND WATCH IT
GROW. FEEL ITS ENERGY.

NOW BREATHE IN ITS LIFE-GIVING
OXYGEN TO COUNTERBALANCE THE
CLIMATE CHANGE THAT'S
SUPPOSEDLY NOT HAPPENING.

TRUMP L'OEIL

HONE YOUR POWERS OF PERCEPTION
TO DECIDE WHAT IS TRUTH AND
WHAT IS NOT FROM THE
STATEMENT BELOW:

'I WILL BUILD A GREAT, GREAT WALL
ON OUR SOUTHERN BORDER, AND I
WILL HAVE MEXICO PAY FOR THAT
WALL. MARK MY WORDS.'

TRUMP CAMPAIGN LAUNCH RALLY
15 JUNE 2015

TRUE   FALSE

INFLATE YOUR EGO

LOOK AT YOURSELF IN THE
MIRROR AND TELL YOURSELF
YOU'RE AWESOME, NO MATTER
HOW IGNORANT, SELFISH OR
RIDICULOUS YOU ARE.

SPEAK YOUR MIND

MAKE AN INSPIRATIONAL SPEECH, SAYING HOW YOU REALLY FEEL.

ALTERNATIVELY JUST COPY WHAT MICHELLE OBAMA SAID.

BE INDEPENDENT

GIVE YOURSELF THE SPACE TO
FORGET ABOUT THE GLOBAL CHAOS
TRUMP WILL CAUSE:

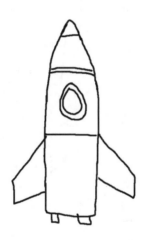

BUILD A ROCKET, SAY GOODBYE TO
THE EARTH, AND SET THE
CONTROLS TO PLUTO!

BE INVENTIVE

THINK OF SOME USES FOR
MIKE PENCE

STAND NEXT TO HIM TO MAKE
YOURSELF LOOK MORE MODERATE.

ORANGE-TINTED SPECTACLES

TRY TO REMEMBER THESE POSITIVES FROM THE PAST THAT HAVE GONE AND SEE IF YOU CAN BRING THAT WARM GLOW INTO YOUR PRSENT...

- ECONOMIC STABILITY

- THE IDEA THAT RACISM AND BIGOTRY IS A BAD THING

- TRUSTING THAT YOUR NEWSFEED IS BASED ON FACT RATHER THAT REVENGE-GENERATING LIES

- A WORLDWIDE AGREEMENT ON CLIMATE CHANGE

- A CONSENSUS ON TRYING TO AVOID WORLD WAR III

- A SANE POTUS

- DECENCY AND GOODWILL TO OTHERS

AMERICA'S NEXT
TOP PRESIDENT

ENGAGE YOUR IMAGINATION BY
ENVISIONING AN UNLIKELIER
PRESIDENT THAN THE DONALD:

HONEY
BOO BOO

ICE CUBE

SKELETOR

LOCKER ROOM TALK

SAY WHAT YOU WANT, ANYTHING GOES, YOU'RE IN THE LOCKER ROOM!

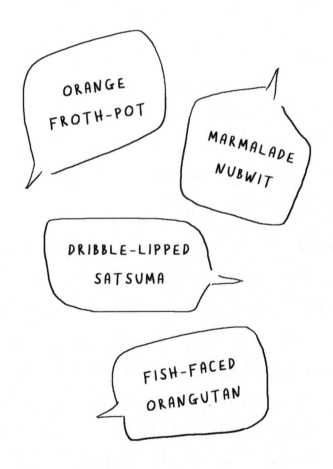

POSITIVITY CALENDAR

MARK OFF EACH DAY OF TRUMP'S
PRESIDENCY. IT WILL BE OVER
BEFORE YOU KNOW IT!

HAPPY ENDING?

HOPEFULLY THIS BOOK HAS GONE SOME WAY TO HELPING YOU ACCEPT THE FACT OF TRUMP'S PRESIDENCY. DONALD'S FOUR YEARS NEED NOT BE A PRISON SENTENCE, UNLESS OF COURSE THE MOST POWERFUL MAN IN THE WORLD DECIDES TO INDICT YOU ON SOME TRUMPED-UP SECURITY BREACH CHARGE?

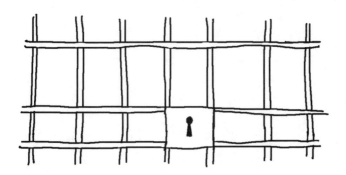

THEN IT WOULD OF COURSE LITERALLY BE A PRISON SENTENCE.